The Lofty Virtues of Shaykh al-Islām Ibn Taymiyyah

Copyright

King Fahd Complex for Printing

Editor/Writer: Noah Ibn Kathir, Imam Ahamd, Imam Al-Qayyim

All rights reserved. No part of this book may be reproduced or transmitted in any form or by any means, electronic or mechanical, including photocopying, recording, or by any information storage and retrieval system, without written permission from the Publisher.

"If I had to swear standing between the corner of the Ka'bah and the spot of Ibrāhīm, I would swear that I have not laid my two eyes on anyone like him, nor has he seen anyone as knowledgeable as himself."

- Al-Hāfidh adh-Dhahabī

Table of Contents

"If you do good in secret, Allah will shower His good on you in public."

Introduction 11

Why I Wrote This Book 21

His Upbringing 24

His Abundant Knowledge, Writings, and Excellent Memory 29

His Knowledge of the Various Types of Related Information 43

His Worship 55

His Cautiousness 65

His Zuhd 69

His Poverty and Humility 75

His Physical Appearance and Dress 85

His Miracles and Incredible Foresight 89

His Generosity 101

His Strength and Bravery 109

His Patience Upon Hardship and Firmness Upon the Truth Until Death 119

Allāh Made Him an Authority and a Clarifier of Truth and Falsehood 125

His Death and the Immense Crowd That Attended His Funeral 133

"What really counts are good endings, not flawed beginnings."-- Ibn Taymiyyah

Books by Ibn Kathir & Ibn Al-Qayyim

"The sinner does not feel any remorse over his sins, that is because his heart is already dead"

* Stories of the Prophets
  ISBN 9798774942602
* Inner Dímensíons of the Salāh
  ISBN 9781643544557
* Seerah of Prophet Mūhammad
  ISBN 9781094860213
* Stories of the Koran
  ISBN 9781095900796
* The Path to Guidance
  ISBN 9781643540818
* Purification of the Soul – Vol 1
  ISBN 9781643541389
* Tafseer Ibn Kathir
  ISBN 9781512266573
* Al-Fawaid: Wise Sayings
  ISBN 9781727812718

* Heaven's Door
  ISBN 9781643541396
* The Ideal Muslimah by *Ibn Kathir*
  ISBN 9798834334422
* Koran: English Easy to Read
  ISBN 9781643540924
* Characteristics of Hypocrites
  ISBN 9781643541358
* Diseases of the Hearts
  and their Cures
  ISBN 9781643541129
* Tawbah: Turning To Allah
  ISBN 979-8517657411
* The Holy Quran – Clear and
    Easy to Read: in English
  ISBN 979851591373
* Timeless Seeds of Advice
  ISBN 9798784652522

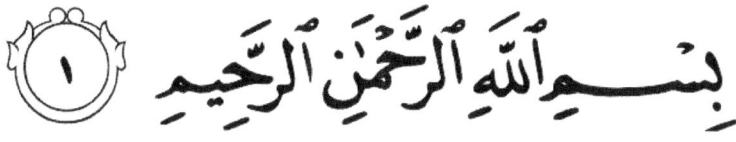

In the name of Allah,

The Entirely Merciful, the Especially Merciful

Indeed, all praise is due to Allāh, Lord of the worlds. We praise Him, seek refuge with Him, and seek His Forgiveness. We seek refuge with Allāh from the evils of our souls (nafs), and the mistakes in our actions. Whoever Allāh Guides, there is none who can misguide him, and whoever Allāh misguides, there is none who can guide him. And I testify that there is none worthy of being worshipped except Allāh, and I testify that Prophet Muhammad, peace and blessings be upon him, is his servant and Last Messenger.

O you who have believed, fear Allah as He should be feared and do not die except as Muslims [in submission to Him]. [3:102]

$$\text{يَٰٓأَيُّهَا ٱلَّذِينَ ءَامَنُوا۟ ٱتَّقُوا۟ ٱللَّهَ حَقَّ تُقَاتِهِۦ وَلَا تَمُوتُنَّ إِلَّا وَأَنتُم مُّسْلِمُونَ ۝}$$

O mankind, fear your Lord, who created you from one soul and created from it its mate and dispersed from both of them many men and women. And fear Allah, through whom you ask one another, and the wombs. Indeed Allah is ever, over you, an Observer. [4:1]

$$\text{يَٰٓأَيُّهَا ٱلنَّاسُ ٱتَّقُوا۟ رَبَّكُمُ ٱلَّذِى خَلَقَكُم مِّن نَّفْسٍ وَٰحِدَةٍ وَخَلَقَ مِنْهَا زَوْجَهَا وَبَثَّ مِنْهُمَا رِجَالًا كَثِيرًا وَنِسَآءً وَٱتَّقُوا۟ ٱللَّهَ ٱلَّذِى تَسَآءَلُونَ بِهِۦ وَٱلْأَرْحَامَ إِنَّ ٱللَّهَ كَانَ عَلَيْكُمْ رَقِيبًا ۝}$$

O you who have believed, fear Allah and speak words of appropriate justice. [33:70]

$$\text{يَٰٓأَيُّهَا ٱلَّذِينَ ءَامَنُوا۟ ٱتَّقُوا۟ ٱللَّهَ وَقُولُوا۟ قَوْلًا سَدِيدًا ۝}$$

He will [then] amend for you your deeds and forgive you your sins. And whoever obeys Allah and His Messenger has certainly attained a great attainment. [33:71]

يُصْلِحْ لَكُمْ أَعْمَٰلَكُمْ وَيَغْفِرْ لَكُمْ ذُنُوبَكُمْ ۗ وَمَن يُطِعِ ٱللَّهَ وَرَسُولَهُۥ فَقَدْ فَازَ فَوْزًا عَظِيمًا ﴿٧١﴾

Indeed, the most truthful of speech is the Speech of Allāh, and the best guidance is the guidance of Prophet Muhammad, peace and blessings be upon him. The worst of affairs are those that are newly introduced, and every newly introduced affair is an innovation, and every innovation is a misguidance, and every misguidance leads to the Fire. Kind speech and forgiveness are better than charity followed by injury. And Allah is Free of need and Forbearing. [2:263]

۞ قَوْلٌ مَّعْرُوفٌ وَمَغْفِرَةٌ خَيْرٌ مِّن صَدَقَةٍ يَتْبَعُهَآ أَذًى ۗ وَٱللَّهُ غَنِىٌّ حَلِيمٌ ﴿٢٦٣﴾

As for what follows: Allāh sent Prophet Muhammad, peace and blessings be upon him, with the pure, easy religion and the comprehensive, inclusive Sharī'ah that brings the human being to the level of perfection, and brings him to the Pleasure of Allāh, and raises his status.

Verily, We have sent you (O Muhammad Peace be upon him) with the truth (Islam), a bringer of glad tidings (for those who believe in what you brought, that they will enter Paradise) and a warner (for those who disbelieve in what you brought, they will enter the Hell-fire). And you will not be asked about the dwellers of the blazing Fire. [2:119]

إِنَّا أَرْسَلْنَاكَ بِالْحَقِّ بَشِيرًا وَنَذِيرًا ۖ وَلَا تُسْأَلُ عَنْ أَصْحَابِ الْجَحِيمِ ۝

And with the help of Allāh, the Prophet, peace and blessings be upon him, sought to lead his nation to Paradise, the abode of peace and security. So, he spent nearly 23 years calling to the message of Islām that Allāh had tasked him with. He faced the horrors he faced for the sake of relaying his message – the message of Islām – in order to leave his nation on the clear path.

And among them are those who abuse the Prophet and say: "He is an ear." Say, "[It is] an ear of goodness for you that believes in Allah and believes the believers and [is] a mercy to those who believe among you." And those who abuse the Messenger of Allah - for them is a painful punishment. [9:61]

وَمِنْهُمُ ٱلَّذِينَ يُؤْذُونَ ٱلنَّبِيَّ وَيَقُولُونَ هُوَ أُذُنٌ قُلْ أُذُنُ خَيْرٍ لَّكُمْ يُؤْمِنُ بِٱللَّهِ وَيُؤْمِنُ لِلْمُؤْمِنِينَ وَرَحْمَةٌ لِّلَّذِينَ ءَامَنُوا۟ مِنكُمْ وَٱلَّذِينَ يُؤْذُونَ رَسُولَ ٱللَّهِ لَهُمْ عَذَابٌ أَلِيمٌ ۝

If we look to the purpose of the message of Islām, we find that it can be summed up in the purifying and nourishing of the soul, and this takes place by knowing and worshipping Allāh, as well as strengthening the ties of brotherhood to spread justice between the slaves of Allāh. The means of doing so is by implementing the teachings of our truthful Prophet, peace and blessings be upon him, which he gathered for us in the treasures and jewels of his Sunnah, his deep words, and what we call Islāmic law (Sharī'ah, or Fiqh).

And the Companions, may Allāh be Pleased with them, exerted their efforts (ijtihād) in deriving rulings in regards to certain matters after the death of our noble Prophet (peace be upon him). Some of them were correct, and others did not arrive at the correct rulings.

These attempts at ijtihād went on, and differing opinions were derived in the name of raising the word of truth and arriving at the highest possible level of perfection (and for Allāh is all perfection). So, the madhāhib were many, and the goal was one.

The result of all this was the authoring of the thousands of books and collections that now fill Islāmic libraries, the raising of the word of truth, and the empowering of the Ummah by its sticking to the religion of truth, Islām. Because of this, all of the powers of the world gathered against the Muslims in order to weaken them. So, the scholars of Islām rose to the occasion and defended Allāh's Religion.

From these scholars who raised the banner of truth and the honor of defending Islām was Shaykh al-Islām Taqī ad-Dīn Ibn Taymiyyah, with the many brave stances he took in his time, and with the countless books and fatāwā of his that now fill the Islāmic library.

And never will the Jews or the Christians approve of you until you follow their religion. Say, "Indeed, the guidance of Allah is the [only] guidance." If you were to follow their desires after what has come to you of knowledge, you would have against Allah no protector or helper. [2:120]

وَلَن تَرْضَىٰ عَنكَ ٱلْيَهُودُ وَلَا ٱلنَّصَٰرَىٰ حَتَّىٰ تَتَّبِعَ مِلَّتَهُمْ ۗ قُلْ إِنَّ هُدَى ٱللَّهِ هُوَ ٱلْهُدَىٰ ۗ وَلَئِنِ ٱتَّبَعْتَ أَهْوَآءَهُم بَعْدَ ٱلَّذِى جَآءَكَ مِنَ ٱلْعِلْمِ ۙ مَا لَكَ مِنَ ٱللَّهِ مِن وَلِىٍّ وَلَا نَصِيرٍ ۝

In order to better know this brave, pious *imām* known as Ibn Taymiyyah, we present to the reader this biography that was written by the pen of a scholar who saw, lived with, and befriended Shaykh al-Islām Ibn Taymiyyah - and he is none other than al-Imām al-Bazzār – and he called this book 'al-A'lām al-'Aliyyah fī Manāqib Ibn Taymiyyah,' and he is the most qualified to write about him.

It is hoped that as opposed to the typical biography that is filled with mere facts and figures, this book will serve to provide the reader with a first-hand account of the human side of one of the greatest Islāmic personalities to have ever lived – one that can be taken as an example in formulating a lifestyle and conducting day to day affairs.

Why I Wrote This Book

"Dhikr (remembrance of Allah) is to the heart as water is to a fish; see what happens to a fish when it is taken out of water"

When I learned of the death of the scholar and educator of this Ummah - the Imām, the mujtahid, the defender of the pure Sharī'ah and Prophetic Sunnah, Shaykh al-Islām Taqī ad-Dīn Abī al-'Abbās Ahmad bin 'Abd al-Halīm bin 'Abd as-Salām bin Taymiyyah (may Allāh sanctify his soul and brighten his grave) - some of the scholars and those who loved good for the Muslims said to me: "You saw and befriended the Shaykh, and you came to know him and his characteristics. If only you could write a few words regarding what you saw in order to benefit whoever of this Ummah comes across them, since mercy descends when we remember the righteous people."

So, I responded: "I only accompanied him for a few days, and I only know few of his many virtues." However, I saw that they intended good and that what they were requesting of me was a right and obligation upon me, as the scholar should be keen to spread and distribute what he thinks will be of value to the Muslims.

So, I produced a small effort describing his virtues which will give the intelligent reader an idea of the honor and excellence of this man. I divided it into sections in order that it be a guide to those who reflect, and I included all that I could remember under each one, covering topics such as:

- His birth and upbringing
- Allāh's leading him to good in his entire life
- His keenness and effort in regards to knowledge
- His constant listening to Ḥadīth
- His numerous written works
- His amazing memory when issuing verdicts and giving lessons
- His stunning expertise in the various types of related information
- His worship and cautiousness
- His zuhd, dedication, and abandonment of the dunyā (life)
- His poverty, humility, generosity, and intelligence
- His firmness, bravery, and patience, and the trials he endured for the Sake of Allāh
- Allāh's Protection for him despite his enemies' envy

- His death, and the immense number of people who prayed at his janāzah
- The love of him that Allāh placed in the hearts of everyone during and after his life
- The spreading of his knowledge and books in the far ends of the Earth

So, I say:

His Upbringing

As for his birth, it is as many of the scholars told narrated to me: he was born in Harrān on the 10th of Rabī' al-Awwal 661 and remained in it until he was seven years old. Then, his father (may Allāh have Mercy on him) took him to Damascus (may Allāh protect it), and he was best upbringing possible there, and Allāh implanted in him the best of traits.

The signs of excellence, dedication, and sharpness were clear in him from an early age. A trustworthy friend who knew him told me that when the Shaykh (may Allah be Pleased with him) was still in the midst of his youth and would to walk to the library, he would be stopped in his path by a Jewish man who lived on the road leading to the library. The Jewish man would ask him about various issues, and would be insistent with his questioning due to Ibn Taymiyyah's intelligence and brightness. Ibn Taymiyyah would answer him so swiftly that the man became fascinated with him. Eventually, whenever Ibn Taymiyyah would come across him, he would provide him with bits of information that would confirm to the man the falsehood he was upon. This went on until he accepted Islām and became a fully practicing Muslim, and this was due to the barakah that the Shaykh had despite his young age.

And since he entered his youth, he spent all of his time engrossed in effort and exertion, and he memorized the entire Qur'ān as a youth, and proceeded to study and memorize Hadīth, Fiqh, and the Arabic language until he excelled at them all. This was in addition to his strict adherence to attending the circles of knowledge and his listening to the narration of Hadīth and āthār. He heard many books from numerous scholars of high caliber. As for the great texts of Islām such as the 'Musnad' of Ahmad, the 'Sahīh's of al-Bukhārī and Muslim, the 'Jāmi'' of at-Tirmidhī, the 'Sunan' of Abū Dāwūd as-Sijistānī, an-Nasā'ī, Ibn Mājah, and ad- Dāraqutnī - he (may Allāh have Mercy on him) had each of them recited to him in their entirety numerous times. The first book that he memorized in Hadīth was al-Humaydī's 'al- Jam' Bayn as-Sahīhayn.'

There was rarely a book in the sciences of Islām except that he would come across it, and Allāh had blessed him with an ability to quickly memorize and rarely forget. He would hardly come across or hear something except that it would remain in his memory, either in wording or meaning. It was as if knowledge had become infused in his flesh, blood, and entire body. He did not merely take pieces of knowledge here and there. Rather, he had complete understanding and comprehension, and was amongst the most outstanding people in virtue and excellence. Allāh tasked him with what would normally destroy anyone else, led him to joy and happiness in all aspects of his life, and made the effects of his leadership from the clearest of signs to all, to the point that everyone with a bit of intelligence agreed that he is from those that the Prophet (peace be upon him) was referring to when he said:

"Indeed, Allāh sends at the beginning of every century he who will revive for this Ummah the affair of its religion," as Allāh has revived through him the laws of this Religion that had long been forgotten, and made him a proof upon all the people of his era, and praise is to Allāh, the Lord of the worlds.

Our Lord, and send among them a messenger from themselves who will recite to them Your verses and teach them the Book and wisdom and purify them. Indeed, You are the Exalted in Might, the Wise. [2:129]

رَبَّنَا وَٱبْعَثْ فِيهِمْ رَسُولًا مِّنْهُمْ يَتْلُواْ عَلَيْهِمْ ءَايَٰتِكَ وَيُعَلِّمُهُمُ ٱلْكِتَٰبَ وَٱلْحِكْمَةَ وَيُزَكِّيهِمْ ۚ إِنَّكَ أَنتَ ٱلْعَزِيزُ ٱلْحَكِيمُ ﴿١٢٩﴾

His Abundant Knowledge, Writings, and Excellent Memory

As for his abundant knowledge, this includes his knowledge of the sciences of the Holy Qur'ān, his ability to derive the smallest and most minute benefits from it, his knowledge of the statements of the scholars in explaining it, his way of using these statements as evidence, as well as the ability Allāh gave him to expose its wonders, the beauty of His legislations, its rare and amazing gems, its linguistic miracles, and its clear grace. In all of this, he was a leader and example that everyone strove to imitate. If someone were to recite some verses of the Mighty Qur'ān in one of his classes, he would proceed to explain them, and his class would end with this.

His class would last for a good portion of the day, and he did not have a designated person to recite for him predetermined verses that he would prepare for. Rather, any random person who was attending his class would recite what was easy for him, and Ibn Taymiyyah would then explain whatever was recited. He would usually not stop except that those in attendance would know that were it not for the lack of time, he would have delved into what he was explaining from many, many more angles. However, he would stop in order to allow his listeners to rest. For example, he delivered a tafsīr of {"Say: 'He is Allāh, One.'"} that took up an entire huge volume. Also, his tafsīr of {"The Beneficent ascended the Throne."} filled around volumes, and I have been told that he began compiling a tafsīr that would have taken up fifty volumes had he completed it.

As for his knowledge and insight into the Sunnah of the Messenger of Allāh (peace be upon him), his statements, actions, life events, battles, armies, the miracles that Allāh granted him, his knowledge of what is authentically narrated from him as opposed to what is unauthentic, as well as the statements, actions, events, and legal verdicts of the Companions (may Allāh be Pleased with them), their struggle for the sake of this Religion, and the virtues that they were granted in exclusion to the rest of the Ummah – in all of this, he was the most precise and had the most expertise, and was the quickest in retrieving whatever information he needed regarding this. He would never mention a hadīth or fatwā that he would use as proof for something except that he would reference it to its proper source in the texts of Islām, or indicate if it was sahīh or hasan, etc., or mention the name of the Companion who narrated it, and he was rarely asked about a narration except that he would clarify its authenticity. And from the most amazing things that occurred is that during his first trial in Egypt, he was taken and jailed such that he was prevented from having access to his books. During this time, he authored many books - small and large - and mentioned in them a great number of ahādīth, narrations, statements of the Companions, names of the scholars of Hadīth, authors, and their works, and he attributed each of these to their proper sources, specifically by name.

He also mentioned the names of the books in which each narration was found, as well as where in the books to find them. All of this was purely from his memory, as at the time he did not have a single book with him to use as a reference.

These books were then published and looked over, and - praise be to Allah - not a single mistake was found in any of them, nor did anything need to be changed in them. And from these books is 'as-Sārim al-Maslūl 'alā Shātim ar-Rasūl,' and this is from the virtue that Allāh - the Exalted - reserved especially for him.

And Allāh also blessed him with the ability to know the differences of opinion amongst the scholars, their statements, their ijtihād in various matters, and what was recorded of the strong, weak, accepted, and rejected opinions of each scholar of each era. He had deep insight into which of their opinions were the most correct and closest to the truth, and was even able to ascribe to each scholar in what location he had come to each opinion.

This was to the point that if he were asked about any of this, it was as if every single saying of the Messenger of Allāh, peace and blessings be upon him, his Companions, and the scholars – from the first of them to the last of them – was a projected image in his mind, with him picking what he wanted and leaving what he wanted. This is something that everyone who ever saw him or came across his knowledge and was not overtaken by ignorance or desires agreed on.

As for his books and writings, they are more than I can mention or think of all their titles. In fact, I doubt that anyone can name them all, as they are many in number, are of varying lengths, and are spread throughout the lands. In fact, I never visited a country except that I saw one of his books in it.

Some of them reached twelve volumes in length, such as 'Talkhīs at-Talbīs 'alā Asās at-Taqdīs,' etc. Some of them are seven volumes long, such as 'al-Jam' Bayn al-'Aql wan-Naql.' Some of them are five volumes long, such as 'Minhāj al-Istiqāmah wal-I'tidāl.'

Some of them are three volumes, such as 'ar-Radd 'alā an-Nasārā.' Some of them are two volumes, such as 'Nikāh al-Muhallal' and 'Ibtāl al-Hayl' and 'Sharh al-'Aqīdah al-Asbahāniyyah.' Some of them are just a single volume or less, and these are too many to encompass. However, I will try my best to mention a few to satisfy the curiosity of those who wish to know: 'Tafsīr Sūrat al-Ikhlās,' his commentary on the verse {"The Beneficent ascended the Throne."}, his book 'as-Sārim al-Maslūl 'alā Shātim ar-Rasūl,' 'al-Furqān al-Mubīn Bayn at-Talāq wal-Yamīn,' 'al-

Furqān Bayn Awliyā' ar-Rahmān wa Awliyā' ash-Shaytān,' 'Iqtidā' as-Sirāt al-Mustaqīm fī Mukhālafat Ashāb al-Jahīm,' 'al-Kalim at-Tayyib,' 'Ithbāt al-Kamāl,' 'ar-Radd 'alā Ta'sīs at-Taqdīs,' 'al-Jam' Bayn al-'Aql wan-Naql,' 'Naqd Aqwāl al-Mubtadi'īn,' 'ar-Radd 'alā an-Nasārā,' 'Minhāj al-Istiqāmah,' 'Ibtāl al-Hayl wa Nikāh al-Muhallal,' 'Sharh al-'Aqīdah

al-Asbahāniyyah,' 'al-Fatāwā,' 'ad-Durr al-Multaqit,' 'Ahkām at-Talāq,' 'ar-Risālah,' 'I'tiqād al-Firqah an-Nājiyah,' 'Raf' al-Malām 'an al-A'immah al-A'lām,' 'Taqrīr Masā'il at-Tawhīd,' 'al-Istighāthah wat-Tawassul,' 'al-Masā'il al-Hamawiyyah,' 'al Masā'il al-Jazriyyah,' and 'al-Masā'il al-Mufradah,' and it is enough to mention these few examples of his writings. Otherwise we would have to list over 200 titles, and this isn't the time or place to do so.

As for his fatāwā and the answers he gave to various questions, these are more than can be counted. However, seventeen volumes of them were compiled and arranged according to Fiqh topics in Egypt, and this is a well-known and famous collection. Also, his companions compiled more than 40,000 issues that he answered.

It was very rare that an event would occur that he was asked about in which he would not reply in the quick and immediate style that he was famous for. This answer would then be turned into a book that anyone else would require a long time sifting through many references to put together, and even then, they would still not match his expertise and efficiency in answering.

I was told by the righteous Shaykh Tāj ad-Dīn Muhammad bin ad-Dawrī that he attended one of Ibn Taymiyyah's classes in which a Jew had asked him about something related to the Qadar. The Jew had presented his question in the form of a poem consisting of eight lines. So, when Ibn Taymiyyah looked at it, he thought to himself for a moment and proceeded to write a reply.

He kept writing, and we thought that he would come out with a scattered, unorganized response. When he finished, his companions looked over what he'd written to find that it was a 184-line poem interspersed within the poem presented by the questioner. His knowledge was so clearly evident in this poem that if one wanted to explain just this poem, he would need to write two large volumes in doing so.

This is just one example of his extraordinary abilities, and how many such answers and fatāwā of his remain unparalleled!

As for his classes, I never missed a single one during my stay in Damascus. He would not prepare anything specifically to present. Rather, he would sit after praying two rak'āt, would praise Allāh, invoke blessings and peace upon His Messenger, peace and blessings be upon him, in a manner so sweet and pleasant that I never heard from anyone else, and would then proceed to speak. Allāh would open up on him such knowledge, gems, hidden benefits, details, narrations, extraction of evidences from verses and ahādīth, statements of the scholars and comparison between them, as well as an ability to supplement what he was saying with old Arabic poetry (and he would sometimes even mention the name of the poem's composer). In all of this, his speech was as smooth as a flowing river, and he would move as the ocean moves. From the beginning of his speech to the end of it, he would appear to be in another world, his eyes closed. This was all done unintentionally, and he didn't try to speak in a certain way to give off this effect. Rather, it was something divine that was evident to everyone who was watching or listening, and he would remain in such a state until he was finished speaking.

I saw him at such times, and he looked like one in the presence of someone preoccupying him from anything else. When he did this, he would have such an amazing presence that it would shake our hearts and grab our attention.

And he would never mention the Messenger of Allāh, peace and blessings be upon him, without invoking peace and blessings on him, and - by Allāh - I never saw anyone who revered the Messenger of Allāh, peace and blessings be upon him, or was keener in imitating him and supporting what he came with than Ibn Taymiyyah. Whenever he came across a hadīth in a particular issue and was sure that it was not abrogated by any other text, he would act upon it and would judge and issue fatāwā accordingly, and would not turn to the statement of any other person, no matter who he was. He (may Allāh be Pleased with him) would say:

"Every person requires proof for his statement, and his statement is not itself a proof, except Allāh and His Messenger, peace and blessings be upon him."

When he finished his class, he would open his eyes and go mix with the people with a cheerful, vibrant face as if he was meeting them for the first time, and he would sometimes even apologize to some of them for what he saw as shortcomings in his talk. Each class he gave in those days took up many notebooks.

What I have mentioned here regarding his classes is something well-known that anyone who attended them would agree on, and such people are many - thanks to Allāh - and their number cannot be calculated: scholars, officials, reciters of the Qur'ān, Muhaddithīn, Fuqahā', poets, and everyday Muslims.

His Knowledge of the Various Types of Related Information

As for his knowledge of both authentic and weak narrations, he was like a mountain in this that nobody could climb. It was very rare that a narration would be mentioned to him without him knowing who said it, who narrated it, who transmitted it, or who recorded it, in addition to knowing the condition of each narrator in light of the sciences of jarh and ta'dīl.

One person who witnessed this describes that he was one day in a class in which a Muhaddith was reading to him from a book of Hadīth. He was reading very fast, and the Shaykh corrected him in the name of a man in the isnād of a hadīth that the reader had sped by, mentioning that his name was such and such as opposed to what was read by the Muhaddith. They looked into it and found that it was exactly as the Shaykh said.

So, look at this swift comprehension and detailed, precise knowledge that nobody can compare to unless they are granted extreme precision!

This is clear as day when looking at the ability Allāh granted him to take the Prophetic narrations and extract concepts and proofs for various issues from them, clarify the intended meanings of their words, explain which narrations specify and restrict the general rulings, point out which narrations are abrogated, delve into the guidelines and principles associated with each narration, explain what each narration implies, and point out what additional knowledge one needed to understand each one – to the point that whenever a verse or hadīth was mentioned to him, he would proceed to bring out from it meanings and concepts that would only be expected from the most amazing of scholars due to how thoroughly he would derive them, and he would mesmerize any who happened to hear him. He was once asked about the hadīth: "Allāh has cursed the one who marries a divorced woman to make her permissible for her first husband, as well as the husband who takes her back."

So, he kept elaborating and explaining to the point that everything he said took up an entire volume. It was quite rare that a hadīth or ruling would be mentioned to him except that he'd spend his entire day explaining it if he wanted to, or that a verse from the Book of Allāh would be mentioned in his presence except that he'd spend the entire gathering explaining it. As for his opposition to the innovators and the people of desires and what he wrote refuting their opinions, exposing their likes, dividing their ranks, cutting off their sustenance, replying to their devilish doubts and opposition to the pure Sharī'ah of Muhammad, peace and blessings be upon him, as well as what Allāh granted him of divine insight, comprehension of the texts, and clear logic that allowed him to remove the mask of falsehood - this is as clear as day. With all that he collected and authored, he clarified the truth from falsehood, to the point that if the followers of this falsehood were alive, they would have no choice but to submit to his words and enter correctly into the Sacred Religion.

Everyone who met him or comes to know of what he had to offer should thank Allāh for leading this Imām to aiding and supporting the truth in such clear and easily understandable manner.

Many famous and virtuous scholars who are known for their expertise in the opinions of the philosophers said that they would be confused between the various opinions of the scholars of Usūl, and that they would not be convinced of one opinion in exclusion to the others, as none of the opinions would seem to contain even a bit of truth. Rather, they would see all of them as being an equal source of confusion and misguidance, and as being too complicated in the proofs and reasoning behind them, and they each feared for themselves from falling into confusion and misguidance because of these opinions.

This was all until Allāh blessed them with the discovery of the books of this Imām, Ahmad bin Taymiyyah, Shaykh al-Islām, and the logical arguments he presented therein. So, all it took was for them to come across his writings and understand them to see that they were in complete agreement with what sound logic would dictate, and this led to the confusion and doubt that had enveloped these scholars from the words of the philosophers completely disappearing.

Whoever wants to verify what I'm saying, let him look without bias, envy, or misguidance to his brief writings in these subjects, such as 'Sharh al-'Aqīdah al-Asbahāniyyah,' etc. If one wishes to also look at this lengthier books, let him read 'Talkhīs at-Talbīs 'alā Asās at-Taqdīs,' 'al-Muwāfaqah Bayn al-'Aql wan-Naql,' or 'Minhāj al-Istiqāmah wal-I'tidāl,' as - by

Allāh - he shines through in these books with the way he clarifies the truth, clings firmly to the clearest of proofs, and weighs his words with the most truthful scale.

He (may Allāh be Pleased with him) wrote a lot about the principles of Islām as opposed to the branches of it. I asked him about this, and requested that he write a Fiqh book compiling all of his chosen and preferred opinions to be a main reference for issuing verdicts.

So, he said: "The branches of the Religion are easy to understand, and it is allowed for whoever follows one of the scholars to simply act on his fatwā as long as there is nothing to make him believe the fatwā to be incorrect.

As for the principles, I see the people of innovation and misguidance - the philosophers, the Bāṭinīs, the heretics, those who believe that Allāh is everywhere, the Dahrīs, the Qadarīs, the Nuṣayrīs, the Jahmīs, the deniers of Allāh's Names and Attributes, those who say He has a physical body, the Mushabbihah, the Rāwindīs, the Kullābīs, the Sulaymīs, and other innovated groups - creating a crisis with their misguidance, and it is clear to me that their intent in this is to destroy the holy Sharī'ah of Muhammad which dominates over all religions, and that most of them dragged the people into doubts regarding the principles of the Religion. Because of this, I rarely see someone turning away from the Qur'ān and Sunnah and going for their opinions except that he becomes a heretic, and falls into doubt of his own religion and beliefs.

When I saw all of this, it became clear to me that whoever is able to repel their doubts and fabrications is to focus all of his efforts in exposing them and responding to their false beliefs in defense of the pure Religion and lofty, authentic Sunnah, and I never saw anyone write regarding this subject who claimed himself to be knowledgeable except that he actually helped demolish the foundations of Islām with his words. This is because of their aversion to the clear truth, their turning away from what the noble Messengers brought from the Lord of the worlds, and their following the path of the philosophers in using their terminology and referring to them as 'wisdoms and logic,' while they are in reality 'stupidity and misguidance.' They stick with this and turn away from everything else until it completely takes over their intellects, and it confuses them until they are no longer able to distinguish between truth and falsehood. Allāh is too generous with His slaves to not provide them with minds that accept the truth and reject falsehood. However, lack of guidance and abundance of desires cause one to fall into misguidance.

Allāh – the Exalted – made the intellect to be a scale for the slave to filter out falsehood from truth, and He did not send the Messengers except to those with intellect, and none are tasked with any obligations except those with intellect and logic, such that he stops and says: 'This contradicts what the noble Messengers conveyed from Allāh.

This is falsehood that anyone with intellect sees,' and whoever is not granted light from Allāh will have no light.

So, this is why I focused all of my attention to writing about the principles of the Religion, and this is what caused me to collect all of their statements and reply to them with what Allāh has blessed me of textual and logical arguments."

I say that in everything he has written, he clarified the truth from falsehood, and Allāh helped him to respond to their innovations, misguided opinions, deceptions, and desires with textual proofs and in a logical manner. He did this to the point that he answered each and every doubt of theirs with such clarity that anyone with a sound mind would understand and agree to his correctness. So, praise be to Allāh who blessed us with the chance to see and befriend him, as Allāh has made him a proof upon the people of his era, most of whom were busy with the worldly pleasures in exclusion to the matters of the Hereafter, and there is no might nor power except with Allāh. However, Allāh - the Mighty and Powerful - guaranteed the preservation of this Religion until the end of time, and made it dominate over all other religions. So, praise be to Allāh, the Lord of the worlds.

His Worship

Seek (beneficial) knowledge, because seeking it for the sake of Allah is a worship. And knowing it makes you more God-fearing; and searching for it is jihad, teaching it to those who do not know is charity, reviewing and learning it more is like tasbeeh. Through knowledge Allah will be known and worshiped.

As for his worship, he (may Allāh be Pleased with him) was unlike anyone else, as he would spend all of his time engrossed in it. He would not let anything - family or wealth - distract him from Allāh. During the nights, he would separate himself from everybody, secluding himself with his Lord, strictly maintaining his recitation of the Mighty Qur'ān, and repeating the various types of daily and nightly worship.

When the night was over, he would rejoin the people for the Fajr prayer, praying the optional prayer before meeting them. When he would begin the prayer, your heart would want to fly from its place just from the way in which he would make the opening takbīr. When he would begin the prayer, his limbs would shake, moving him left and right. When he would recite, he would elongate his recitation just as was authentically reported regarding the recitation of the Messenger of Allāh (peace be upon him).

His bowing, prostration, and his coming up from them were from the most complete of what has ever been reported in regards to the obligatory prayer. He would severely lighten his sitting for the first tashahhud, and would say the first taslīm out loud to the point that everyone who was present would hear it.

When he finished his prayer, he and whoever was present would praise Allāh with what was narrated: 'Oh Allāh, You are Peace, and You are the Source of Peace. You are Blessed, O Possessor of Glory and Honor,' and he would then turn to the congregation, repeat the narrated tahlīl, as well as the tasbīh, tahmīd, and takbīr, and complete the hundred with a tahlīl as was narrated, and the congregation would do exactly as he did. He would then supplicate to Allāh for himself and the Muslims with the various narrated supplications, and he would most often supplicate with:

'O Allāh! Aide us and do not aide anyone over us. Plan for us and not against us. Guide us and make guidance easy for us. O Allāh! Make us thankful to You, depending on and remembering You, submissive to You, loving You, fearing

You, and obedient to You. Our Lord! Accept our repentance, wash away our sins, and keep our words firm. Guide our hearts, and remove all malice from our chests,' and he would open and close this supplication by praying for the Prophet (peace be upon him), and he would then proceed to engage in dhikr.

And I came to know that it was his habit that nobody would speak to him unless absolutely necessary after the Fajr prayer. He would remain in a state of dhikr of Allāh, listening to himself. Sometimes, he would let those sitting next to him listen to his dhikr, all the while constantly turning his eyesight to the sky.

He would remain in such a state until the Sun rose and the time in which prayer is forbidden had passed.

During my stay in Damascus, I would spend some of the day and most of the night with him. He would draw me near to him, sitting me beside him. I would hear what he would recite and repeat, and I saw that he would repeat 'al-Fātihah' over and over again, and would spend all of his time between Fajr and sunrise doing this. So, I kept thinking to myself, wondering why he would recite this specific chapter of the Qur'ān in exclusion to the others. Eventually, it became clear to me - and Allāh Knows best - that his intention in doing so was to combine with his recitation between what was narrated in the ahādīth and what was discussed by the scholars in regards to whether the narrated adhkār should take precedence over recitation of the Qur'ān or vice versa.

So, he saw that in repeating 'al-Fātiḥah,' he could combine between both opinions and reap the benefits of both actions, and this was from his strength in logic and depth of insight. After this, he would pray Duḥā, and if he wanted to hear Ḥadīth in another place, he would rush to that place with whoever happened to be with him at the time. It was rare that any intelligent person would see him and not come and kiss his hands. Even the busiest of businessmen would walk from what they were doing to greet him and seek his blessings. With all of this, he would give every one of them their share of attention, greetings, etc. And when you are greeted with a greeting, greet [in return] with one better than it or [at least] return it [in a like manner]. Indeed, Allah is ever, over all things, an Accountant. [4:86]

وَإِذَا حُيِّيتُم بِتَحِيَّةٍ فَحَيُّوا بِأَحْسَنَ مِنْهَا أَوْ رُدُّوهَا ۗ إِنَّ ٱللَّهَ كَانَ عَلَىٰ كُلِّ شَىْءٍ حَسِيبًا ۝

If he saw any evil in the street, he would work to remove it, and if he heard of a funeral taking place, he would rush to pray in it or apologize for missing it. Sometimes, he would go to the grave of the deceased after he finished listening to Hadīth and pray over it. Afterwards, he would return to his mosque, where he would remain either giving fatāwā to the people or fulfilling their needs until it was time to pray Dhuhr in congregation. He would spend the rest of the day in such a manner. His classes were open to the general public: for the old, the young, the wealthy, the poor, the free, the slave, males, and females. He attracted everyone that would pass by him, and every one of them would feel that Ibn Taymiyyah was treating them better than he was treating anyone else present. He would then pray Maghrib and follow it up with as much optional prayer as Allāh made possible.

I or someone else would then read his writings to him, and he would benefit us with various points and notes. We would do this until we prayed 'Ishā', after which we would continue as we were before, delving into the various fields of knowledge. We would do this until much of the night had passed. During this entire time - night and day - Ibn Taymiyyah would constantly remember Allāh, mention His Oneness, and seek His Forgiveness.

And he would constantly raise his eyesight to the sky and would not stop doing this, as if he saw something there that kept his eyesight hooked. He would do this for as long as I was staying with him.

So, subhān Allāh! How short were these days! If only they were longer! By Allāh, until this day, there has never been a time in my life that was more beloved to me than the time I spent with him, and I was never seen in a better state than I was at that time, and this was for no other reason than the barakah of the Shaykh, may Allāh be Pleased with him. Every week, he would visit the sick, especially those at the hospital, and I have been informed by more than one person whose trustworthiness I do not doubt that the entire life of the Shaykh was spent in the way that I witnessed and described above. So, what worship, and what jihād, is better than this?

Indeed, Allah is my Lord and your Lord, so worship Him. That is the straight path. [3:51]

إِنَّ ٱللَّهَ رَبِّي وَرَبُّكُمْ فَٱعْبُدُوهُ ۚ هَٰذَا صِرَٰطٌ مُّسْتَقِيمٌ ﴿٥١﴾

Some people have the disease of criticizing all the time. They forget the good about others and only mention their faults. They are like flies that avoid the good and pure places and land on the bad and wounds. This is because of the evil within the self and the spoiled nature

-- Ibn Taymiyyah

His Cautiousness

He (may Allāh be Pleased with him) was an example of the peak of cautiousness, as Allāh caused him to spend his entire life in a state of cautiousness. He never mixed with the people for the purpose of buying, selling, transaction, business, partnership, agriculture, or ownership, nor was he made to watch over any wealth, nor did he ever accept a gift or offer from a ruler, governor, or businessman, nor did he save up any money of his own. Rather, the only thing he produced during his life, and the only thing he left to be inherited after his death, was knowledge. He did this in imitation of the leader of the Messengers and the seal of the Prophets, Muhammad (peace be upon him, his Household, and Companions), who said:

"Indeed, the scholars are the inheritors of the Prophets, and the Prophets did not leave behind a dīnār or dirham to be inherited. Rather, they left behind knowledge to be inherited, and whoever takes from it has acquired a great fortune." And he used to encourage the intelligent people around him - in the most pleasant and concise manner - to choose their path and follow in their footsteps, even if taking an easier path was technically permissible. However, the smart one is he who is driven to achieve the best. As for those who strive hard in Us (Our Cause), We will surely guide them to Our Paths, Allah's Religion, And verily, Allah is with the Muhsinun (good doers). [26:69]

وَٱلَّذِينَ جَٰهَدُوا۟ فِينَا لَنَهْدِيَنَّهُمْ سُبُلَنَا وَإِنَّ ٱللَّهَ لَمَعَ ٱلْمُحْسِنِينَ ﴿٦٩﴾

So, look to how Allāh led this Imām to avoid all except what he needed in life. He was overtaken by his love for Allāh, and as a result was granted all virtue and excellence as opposed to the scholars of the dunyā who choose it, seek it, and chase after it. When they chose its delights, they closed themselves off from the path of guidance, and as a result fell into its opposite. They go about in a state of confusion, just like the one walking around in the darkness, not knowing what they are eating or wearing. They do not even know what they hope to achieve from their evil and humiliating aims. They compete for them, envy each other because of them, fill their bodies with them, and push everything else out of their hearts. They tend excessively to their outer appearances while their hearts are blackened and corrupted. They are never satisfied until they become enemies to those who reject and hate such a lifestyle.

When they saw this Imām as a scholar of the Hereafter - abandoning their habits of gathering the goods of this world, avoiding the doubtful, and rejecting the unnecessary permissible things - they came to see that his mannerisms exposed and embarrassed them. So, they became extremely jealous that he displayed such spiritual characteristics while they had nothing but devilish ones, and they conspired to ruin him wherever they could, forgetting that they were foxes while he was a lion. So, Allāh protected him from them in more than one instance, just as He always does with His beloved servants. He protected him for the duration of his life, and spread his knowledge after his death to the ends of the Earth. And of the people is he who sells himself, seeking means to the approval of Allah. And Allah is kind to [His] servants. [2:207]

وَمِنَ ٱلنَّاسِ مَن يَشْرِى نَفْسَهُ ٱبْتِغَآءَ مَرْضَاتِ ٱللَّهِ وَٱللَّهُ رَءُوفٌ بِٱلْعِبَادِ ۝

His Zuhd

As for his zuhd from the world and its delights, Allāh made this a constant theme in his life from the time of his youth. A trustworthy friend narrated to me that his teacher who taught Ibn Taymiyyah the Qur'ān said:

"His father said to me while he was still a young boy: "I would like for you to promise him that if he does not stop reciting and practicing Qur'ān, I will give him forty dirhams every month." So, he gave me the forty dirhams, and told me: "Give them to him. He is young, and he might become happy and increase in his zeal to memorize and learn the Qur'ān, and tell him that he will have the same every month."

Those to whom We have given the Quran recite it with its true recital. They [are the ones who] believe in it. And whoever disbelieves in it - it is they who are the losers. [2:121]

$$ ٱلَّذِينَ ءَاتَيْنَٰهُمُ ٱلْكِتَٰبَ يَتْلُونَهُۥ حَقَّ تِلَاوَتِهِۦٓ أُو۟لَٰٓئِكَ يُؤْمِنُونَ بِهِۦ ۗ وَمَن يَكْفُرْ بِهِۦ فَأُو۟لَٰٓئِكَ هُمُ ٱلْخَٰسِرُونَ ﴿١٢١﴾ $$

And how could you disbelieve while to you are being recited the verses of Allah and among you is His Messenger? And whoever holds firmly to Allah has [indeed] been guided to a straight path. [3:101]

$$ وَكَيْفَ تَكْفُرُونَ وَأَنتُمْ تُتْلَىٰ عَلَيْكُمْ ءَايَٰتُ ٱللَّهِ وَفِيكُمْ رَسُولُهُۥ ۗ وَمَن يَعْتَصِم بِٱللَّهِ فَقَدْ هُدِىَ إِلَىٰ صِرَٰطٍ مُّسْتَقِيمٍ ﴿١٠١﴾ $$

They are not [all] the same; among the People of the Scripture is a community standing [in obedience], reciting the verses of Allah during periods of the night and prostrating [in prayer]. [3:113]

> ۞ لَيْسُوا۟ سَوَآءً ۗ مِّنْ أَهْلِ ٱلْكِتَٰبِ أُمَّةٌ قَآئِمَةٌ يَتْلُونَ ءَايَٰتِ ٱللَّهِ ءَانَآءَ ٱلَّيْلِ وَهُمْ يَسْجُدُونَ ۝

Ibn Taymiyyah refused to accept any money, saying: "O teacher, I promised Allāh that I would not take any payment for the Qur'ān," and he never accepted them. I thought to myself that this would never occur except from a youth who is preserved by Allāh."

This teacher has spoken the truth, as the protection and attention of Allāh is what brought him all the good in his life from beginning to end. Everyone who ever met him - especially those who accompanied him for extended periods of time - agrees that they never saw anyone equal to him in his zuhd of the dunyā, to the point that he became famous for this, and this became known in the heart of everyone who heard of his characteristics, far and near. In fact, if you were to ask an everyday person living here who wasn't too close to the Shaykh:

'Who was the person who displayed the most zuhd of our times, and was the strongest in rejecting the unnecessary things of this dunyā, and the keenest of them in seeking the Hereafter?' he would say: 'I never heard of anyone like Ibn Taymiyyah (may Allāh have Mercy on him)!'

He did not become famous for this except because of his dedication in doing so. How many scholars have we seen who are as satisfied with what little portion of the dunyā they have like he was? He was never heard asking for a beautiful wife, or an enchanting slave girl, or a well-built house, or obedient slaves, or plush gardens, or a strong riding beast, or soft and elegant clothing, or a position of leadership, nor did he ever hold back a dīnār or dirham, nor was he ever seen striving to obtain something permissible and unnecessary. This was all despite the fact that kings, governors, and well-known businessmen were all under his command, submissive to his words, willing to come close to him as much as they were able, openly praising of him, and each ready to take care of his financial needs.

So, where is he in comparison to some who ascribe themselves to knowledge while they are not from its people - those who were fooled by Satan into submitting to him in word and deed? Do you not see that they looked to their characteristics and his, their virtues and his, their envy in competing over the dunyā and his complete disregard for them, their rush to gather as much as they could of it and his rush to escape from it, their servitude to the rulers and constant presence at their doors compared to the rulers' submission to him, his lack of intimidation by their authority and power, the ease with which he would speak the truth to them, and the force with which he would address them? Indeed, by Allāh! However, they shaved themselves - of their religion, not their hair, and the love of the dunyā overtook their dreams, and they were robbed - of their intellect, not their possessions, to the point that they would turn away from those who came to ask it of them, and would only befriend those who would help them get more of it.

His Poverty and Humility

With his extreme abandonment and rejection of the dunyā and his possession only of the small amount that he happened to come across of it, he (may Allāh be Pleased with him) would never belittle the smallest things or be distracted by the most valuable things to give it away in charity. And be steadfast in prayer and regular in charity: And whatever good ye send forth for your souls before you, ye shall find it with Allah: for Allah sees Well all that ye do. [2:110]

وَأَقِيمُواْ ٱلصَّلَوٰةَ وَءَاتُواْ ٱلزَّكَوٰةَ وَمَا تُقَدِّمُواْ لِأَنفُسِكُم مِّنْ خَيْرٍ تَجِدُوهُ عِندَ ٱللَّهِ إِنَّ ٱللَّهَ بِمَا تَعْمَلُونَ بَصِيرٌ ۝

He would always give charity to the point that if he could find nothing to give, he would take off a portion of what he was wearing to give it to the poor.

He would sometimes take one or two loaves of bread from the already meager provision he had and hide them under his sleeve, and when we went out with him to listen to Hadīth, he would rush to give them to some poor person when he thought we weren't watching. At other times, if a poor person came to him and stood with him for some time, he would sit him down and give him most of his food. *Those who (in charity) spend of their goods by night and by day, in secret and in public, have their reward with their Lord: on them shall be no fear, nor shall they grieve.* [2:274]

$$ ٱلَّذِينَ يُنفِقُونَ أَمْوَٰلَهُم بِٱلَّيْلِ وَٱلنَّهَارِ سِرًّا وَعَلَانِيَةً فَلَهُمْ أَجْرُهُمْ عِندَ رَبِّهِمْ وَلَا خَوْفٌ عَلَيْهِمْ وَلَا هُمْ يَحْزَنُونَ ﴿٢٧٤﴾ $$

I was told by the righteous Shaykh Zayn ad-Dīn 'Alī al-Wāsitī, who stayed with the Shaykh for a long time:

"We would usually get our food at the beginning of the day, and it would consist of a piece of bread that weighed about half an Iraqi ratl. So, he would break a piece off with his hand, and we would eat from it together. He would raise his hands from the bread before me, and would not remove the rest of the piece from in front of me until I was full. I would not need any food until nighttime, and I saw that this was from the barakah of the Shaykh. We would then stay until the last part of the night after he finished all of his daily tasks of helping the people, and we would then be given supper. He would eat a few pieces with me, and leave me to finish the rest. I would ask him to eat more and he would refuse, to the point that I would be pained due to how little he would eat. This was our routine for the majority of the time I stayed with him, and I never saw myself more fulfilled and content than I was at that time, and I also never lived in more poverty than I did at that time." And many people describe the concern for the poor and needy that he was famous for, as well as for the needy scholars, and his efforts in helping them out. In fact, he would lend a helping hand to every type of person he was able to do some good for.

As for his humility, I never saw or heard of anyone in his time to equal him in this. He was humble with the old and the young, the respected and the belittled, the pious rich and the poor. He would honor the pious poor and treat them in a respectable, simple way, and would speak to them with sweeter words than would be used with the rich. He would even serve them with his own hands, carrying their belongings in order to get closer to his Lord.

He would never appear tired in front of anyone who came to ask him a question. Rather, he would greet the questioner with a pleasant face and stand with him until he was the one who proceeded to leave - whether such a person was old or young, a man or a woman, a free man or a slave, a scholar or a layman, a city resident or a bedouin. He would not embarrass them, make them uncomfortable, or rush them. Rather, he would answer them, make sure they understood his answer, and clarify what was correct from what was incorrect, all with softness and simplicity. Allah brings (the) Wisdom to whomever He decides; and whoever is brought (the) Wisdom, then he has been brought much charity (i.e., benefit); and in no way does anyone constantly remember except the ones endowed with intellects. [2:269]

يُؤْتِى ٱلْحِكْمَةَ مَن يَشَآءُ وَمَن يُؤْتَ ٱلْحِكْمَةَ فَقَدْ أُوتِىَ خَيْرًا كَثِيرًا وَمَا يَذَّكَّرُ إِلَّآ أُوْلُواْ ٱلْأَلْبَٰبِ ﴿٢٦٩﴾

He was humble with people whether they were present or absent, whether he was standing or sitting, and whether he was walking in the street or sitting in a gathering. He was excessively generous and humble with me during my stay with him, to the point that he would not even address me by my first name! He would instead give me the best of nicknames. He would especially be generous and treat me with great respect in front of my own companions, such that he would never let me sit except at his side, whether the gathering was lengthy or short, public or private. He would always be by my side during my reading of 'Saḥīḥ al-Bukhārī,' despite the fact that I had intended to have it read privately due to how little I thought of myself to read it in front of the people, and because I wanted to take advantage of the free time out of fear that the teacher who was reading it with me would have to leave, since he was one of the few narrators of 'Saḥīḥ al-Bukhārī' who had heard it from the companions of Abī al-Waqt as-Sajzī.

So, when the Shaykh heard of this, he made me read it in front of a large group of people - men, women, and children - and said: "This should never be done except in a way that will benefit the Muslims," and he spent all of his time with me, such that I achieved what I wanted and more in only twenty sessions. We met every day except Friday, and he would be with me every step of the way, attending the sessions with his own copy in hand that was from the original manuscript of al-Ḥāfidh Ibn Nāsir and using it to keep my teacher in check, as the Shaykh's copy was more accurate.

His beautiful manners were further manifestation of his intense humility, such that when we would leave his house to read, he would carry our books himself and would not let anyone else carry them, and I would apologize to him for this out of fear of appearing to have bad manners. He would then say: "If I were to carry it on my head, my head would not be deserving of carrying something that contained the words of the Messenger, peace and blessings be upon him!"

When I would read to the class, he would sit under the chair, avoiding the center of the gathering. This would cause me to be extremely shy from sitting with him, and I would be amazed at his intense humility and excess in honoring me in a way I did not deserve, and how he would elevate me in front of everyone. Were it not for the fact that I was reading the words of the Messenger, peace and blessings be upon him, and considering their sacredness and honor, there would have been no reason for him to act this way. This level of humility and generosity was his habit with all who came into contact with him or befriended him, such that everyone who met him later described his excess humility just like I have and more. So, Glorified is the One who gave him this, and may He reward him for all the good he has done. And lower to them the wing of humility out of mercy and say: My Lord, have mercy upon them as they brought me up [when I was] small. [17:24]

وَٱخْفِضْ لَهُمَا جَنَاحَ ٱلذُّلِّ مِنَ ٱلرَّحْمَةِ وَقُل رَّبِّ ٱرْحَمْهُمَا كَمَا رَبَّيَانِي صَغِيرًا ﴿٢٤﴾

Those who love their Lord are not too proud to serve Him, and they declare His glory and prostrate in humility before Him. [7:206]

إِنَّ ٱلَّذِينَ عِندَ رَبِّكَ لَا يَسْتَكْبِرُونَ عَنْ عِبَادَتِهِۦ وَيُسَبِّحُونَهُۥ وَلَهُۥ يَسْجُدُونَ ۩ ﴿٢٦﴾

And so those who were given knowledge may know that it is the truth from your Lord and [therefore] believe in it, and their hearts humbly submit to it. And indeed is Allah the Guide of those who have believed to a straight path. [22:54]

وَلِيَعْلَمَ ٱلَّذِينَ أُوتُوا۟ ٱلْعِلْمَ أَنَّهُ ٱلْحَقُّ مِن رَّبِّكَ فَيُؤْمِنُوا۟ بِهِۦ فَتُخْبِتَ لَهُۥ قُلُوبُهُمْ وَإِنَّ ٱللَّهَ لَهَادِ ٱلَّذِينَ ءَامَنُوٓا۟ إِلَىٰ صِرَٰطٍ مُّسْتَقِيمٍ ﴿٥٤﴾

And the slaves of the Most Beneficent (Allah) are those who walk on the earth in humility and sedateness, and when the foolish address them (with bad words) they reply back with mild words of gentleness. [25:63]

وَعِبَادُ ٱلرَّحْمَٰنِ ٱلَّذِينَ يَمْشُونَ عَلَى ٱلْأَرْضِ هَوْنًا وَإِذَا خَاطَبَهُمُ ٱلْجَٰهِلُونَ قَالُوا۟ سَلَٰمًا ﴿٦٣﴾

His Physical Appearance and Dress

"When someone offends me, I think it is a gift from Allah (god). He (Allah) is teaching me humility."

He was moderate in his appearance and dress. He would not wear extravagant clothes that attracted attention or made him look special. Rather, his clothing and appearance were just like that of the general people, and he did not wear one particular type of clothing in exclusion to another.

He would wear whatever was available, and he would eat whatever was made available to him, and the badhādhah (plain appearance) of faith was evident on him. He was never seen showing off with his turban, his clothing, his manner of walking, or how he stood and sat, and he never dressed up for anyone who he was meeting or was visiting him from another land.

And what amazed me was that I had a dream long before I ever met him in which he and I were sitting and eating some food in a certain manner. When we finally met, I saw him eating that same food in the exact manner that I had seen in the dream. He sat me down, and we likewise ate together just as I saw in the dream! And many people told me that he was never seen or heard asking for food - dinner or supper - no matter how long he remained busy with some matter related to knowledge and deed. Rather, he would sometimes be given food that he would leave for a long time before even turning to it, and if he ate from it, would only eat small bits. He would never mention the delights of this world, and would never speak or ask about them. Rather, all of his concern and conversation was in seeking the Hereafter and what could bring him closer to Allāh, the Exalted.

This is exactly how he was in how he dressed. He was never heard asking for a particular type of clothing. Rather, his family would bring him some clothes whenever they knew that he needed to change the clothes he was wearing.

He would maybe even keep one set of clothes on for so long that they became dirty, and he would not ask anyone to wash them for him, and it was his family who would ask if he needed them washed. His brother - who was the one looking after his worldly interests - told me: "This was how he was in his food, drink, clothing, and whatever else he needed from the worldly matters."

And I never saw anyone who respected and revered the Shaykh more than this brother of his.

His brother would sit in his presence as if there was a bird on his head, and he would respect him as one would respect a ruler. We were amazed at this, and said to him: "Usually, a man's family does not treat him in the same way that a stranger would. They usually treat him in a less formal way, and we see you with the Shaykh as if you are his student with all the respect and honor in which you deal with him." So, he would say: "I see things from him that nobody else sees, and it is therefore a must that I treat him as you see." When we asked him what it was he would see, he would refuse to answer due to how much he knew the Shaykh would hate that.

His Miracles and Incredible Foresight

The sincere hearts and the pious supplications are soldiers which can never be defeated

Many trustworthy individuals narrated to me various miracles that they witnessed from him, and I will mention some of them here, beginning with two that I personally witnessed.

There was once an argument between some of the noble scholars and myself in some issues that we were debating at length over. So, we decided to stop our discussion and go to the Shaykh to give us the decisive word. We found that the Shaykh himself had come to us, and when we were going to ask him about what we were discussing, he delved into each issue before we could even speak.

He laid out each of our positions about what we were discussing, mentioned the opinions of the scholars on them, and then clarified which opinions were most supported by the evidence, until he got to the final issue we wanted to ask him about and told us what we ourselves were hoping to learn from asking him. So, my companions and I were speechless and shocked at what he had just learned from him, as well as what Allāh had made him privy to regarding what we had been thinking of.

And during the days I spent with him, if I wanted to research a particular issue, I would barely have just thought of it only to find him proceeding to explaining it to me, and giving me an answer from many angles.

The righteous, knowledgeable Shaykh Ahmad bin al-Harīmī told me that he once traveled to Damascus. He said: "So, it happened that when I arrived, I had no provision or money with me, and I knew nobody in the city. So, I began to walk through its streets like a lost person. Suddenly, I saw the Shaykh walking swiftly towards me. He greeted me, smiled in my face, put in my hand a small pouch filled with some dirhams, and said to me: "Spend these now and stop worrying about what you are thinking about, as Allāh will never abandon you."

He then walked away as if he had only come to say this to me. So, I supplicated for him, and I was very happy with this. I then asked some of the people: "Who is this man?" They said: "You don't know him?! He is Ibn Taymiyyah!

It has been a very long time since we've seen him walk this road." The best part of my visit to Damascus was this instance where I met him, as Allāh was the One who caused us to cross paths. I did not need anyone else for anything during the remainder of my stay in Damascus, as Allāh had provided for me from where I did not expect. Later on, I decided to visit him again, and he would honor me and ask how I was doing, and I would praise Allāh in response to him."

And I was told by Shaykh Taqī ad-Dīn 'Abdullāh bin Ahmad bin Sa'īd: "I traveled to Egypt when the Shaykh was living there, and I became very sick the night I arrived. So, I spent the night in some region of the country, and was shocked to suddenly hear someone calling me by my name and nickname.

So, I answered him in a weak voice, and I sat up to see a group of the Shaykh's companions entering upon me, some of whom I had met previously in Damascus. I said: "How did you know I was coming to Egypt when I have just arrived?" They said: "The Shaykh informed us that you were coming and that you are sick, and he told us to hurry to move you somewhere more comfortable, and we saw nobody else arriving or telling us anything." So, I know that this was from the miracles of the Shaykh (may Allāh be Pleased with him). He also told me: "I became extremely sick in Damascus, such that I could not even sit up. I suddenly felt the Shaykh sitting next to my head, and I was very weak with fever and sickness. He supplicated for me and said: "You are now relieved." As soon as he left me, I was immediately relieved of all the pain and sickness I had been experiencing."

He also said: "I had come across some poetry written by one who had strayed from the truth that attacked the Shaykh. The reason he had written this poem was that someone had ascribed to him poetry and words that indicated he was a Rāfidī, and took these words to a judge, and it was decided to publicize his condition to the people.

The man falsely thought that it was the Shaykh who had written these words and taken them to the judge, and this is why he wrote this poetry attacking the Shaykh. So, I kept this poem with me, and I would sometimes recite some of it. I came across many things in it that didn't sit well, and I was constantly afraid and anxious because of what I was reading, and were it not for Allāh's blessing on me, I would have been overtaken by it.

I asked myself why I was so affected by this poem, and I could find nothing more than that I liked some of its words. So, I promised Allāh that I would not waste any more time reading it, and I became a bit relieved and relaxed. But, I still had the poem. So, I took it and burned it up and washed away the ashes so that nothing would be left of it.

I asked Allāh's Forgiveness, and suddenly was completely relieved of all the anxiety I had been feeling when reading the poem, and Allāh replaced it with relaxation.

I have since been in a state of good and relaxation, and I see that this was one of the miracles of the Shaykh granted to him by Allāh."

He also said to me that Shaykh Ibn 'Imād ad-Dīn al-Muqri' al-Mutriz said: "I visited the Shaykh once when I had some money with me. I greeted him, and he replied and welcomed me, and then left me without asking if I had any money with me. After a few days, I had spent all of my money. When the class was over and we had prayed behind him, he wouldn't let me leave. He sat me down, and after everyone had left, he put a small pouch of money in my hand, saying: "Now, you have no money. Support yourself with this." I was amazed at this, and knew that Allāh had somehow made him privy to my situation - both when I had some money and when I had run out of it."

I was also informed by a trustworthy individual: "When the Mongol invasion was approaching Damascus, its people became extremely afraid, and some of them came to him and asked him to supplicate for the Muslims. So, he turned to Allāh and then said: "Rejoice, for Allāh will grant you victory in three days, to the point that you will see their heads piled on top of each other." By the One in Whose Hand my soul is, as soon as three days had passed, we saw their heads piled on top of each other in the center of Damascus, just as he said."

And I was told by the righteous Shaykh 'Uthmān bin Ahmad bin 'Īsā an-Nassākh (may Allāh be Pleased with him) that he would visit the sick in the hospital in Damascus every week, and this was a constant habit of his. He once came to a young man and supplicated for him, and he was quickly cured.

He came to the Shaykh wanting to greet him, and when he saw him, he smiled to him, pulled him close, gave him some money, and said: "Allāh has healed you. So, promise Him that you will quickly return to your homeland. Is it right for you to abandon your wife and four daughters without a provider while you sit here?" The man kissed his hand and said: "Sir, I repent to Allāh on your hand," and he later said: "I was amazed at what he knew about me, as I did leave them without any provision, and nobody in Damascus had known of my situation."

And I was told by someone I trust that some judges were on their way to Egypt to assume positions there, and that one of them said: "As soon as I arrive in Egypt, I will rule that such and such of the noble scholars should be killed."

Everyone had agreed that this scholar was righteous and pious. However, this man's heart contained such hatred and enmity to him that it drove him to want him dead. Everyone who heard him say this became worried that he would actually carry out his threat to kill this righteous man, and they were afraid that this man who wanted to be a judge would be led by Satan and by his own desires, causing him to spill sacred Muslim blood - they feared the great evil that would result from such an action.

So, they went to Ibn Taymiyyah and told him of exactly what had taken place. He said: "Allāh will not allow him to carry out what he wants, and he will not even get to Egypt alive." The judge had a very short distance to travel until he would arrive in Egypt when he was suddenly stricken with death.

So, he died before arriving in Egypt, just as Allāh had revealed on the tongue of the Shaykh (may Allāh be Pleased with him). And the miracles of the Shaykh (may Allāh be Pleased with him) are many, and this is not the place to mention more of them. But, from the most obvious and well-known of his miracles is that nobody was ever known to hate or attack him except that he was then stricken with numerous disasters, mostly in his religion, and this is something well-known that does not require much elaboration.

His Generosity

Religion revolves around knowing the truth and acting by it, and action must be accompanied by patience

He (may Allāh be Pleased with him) was a naturally generous person, and did not have to change himself to become so. I mentioned previously that he never held back a bit of money. Rather, he would give away whatever he could, and would never turn away someone who came to ask of him something that he owned, whether this was a dirham or dīnār, some clothing, books, etc. In fact, he was sometimes approached by a needy person when he had nothing with him to give away, and because he didn't want to turn him away empty handed, he would remove something he was wearing and give it to him. This is something that everyone knew of him.

I was told by Shaykh Taqī ad-Dīn 'Abdullāh bin Ahmad bin Sa'īd: "I was sitting with Shaykh al-Islām Ibn Taymiyyah one day, and a person came and greeted him. The Shaykh saw that he was in need of something to wrap his head with. So, without the man even asking, he took off his turban, cut it in half, wrapped his head with one half, and gave the other half to the man." It might be that some who lack understanding see that this constituted a waste of money on the part of the Shaykh, or was a type of sacrifice that detracted from his manhood, and this is not at all the case. He possessed nothing but his clothes, and he saw that if he took off anything but his turban, this would harm him and not be in anyone's interests, and he did not own at the time any other clothing that he did not need and could give away.

So, he rushed to cut off a piece of what he didn't wholly need, and ended up simultaneously benefiting his Muslim brother with part of it and himself with the rest of it. This is the best and smartest way of dealing with such situations, and this is the generosity that he became famous for.

As for the form of charity that might constitute a reduction in manhood, this has nothing to do with what happened. Rather, this is from his intense humility, not seeing himself as being great, and not wanting to elevate himself in front of those present, and this is a praiseworthy characteristic that is required according to both religion and logic.

And a similar example was related from the leader of humanity and the best of them in manners, manhood, intellect, and knowledge, Muhammad the Mustafā (peace be upon him). It was narrated that he came out to the mosque wearing a black cloak with white borders while a group of Muslims were present. So, one of them saw him and said: "O Messenger of Allāh! Give me this cloak!" And he (peace be upon him) never refused anyone's request. So, he took off the cloak and gave it to the man out of generosity. The people then began criticizing the man for what he did, since the Prophet, peace and blessings be upon him, needed what he was wearing, and it was known that he never refused a request. So, the man apologized to them and said: "I did not ask for it so that I would wear it. Rather, I want to be shrouded in it when I die," and the narrator of the story says that he actually did hold onto it until he died and was buried in it.

This hadīth is well-known, and it was reported by many trustworthy narrators, and it is from the clearest of proofs for what we have said. He went above and beyond in generosity and humility, breaking his ego, and displaying beautiful manners. I was told by a trustworthy friend that the Shaykh was once walking through the streets, and one of the poor called out to him. He knew that he was needy, and had nothing to give them. So, he took off some of the clothing he was wearing and gave it to him, saying: "This is all I have, and I am sorry that I have nothing more to give you."

Those who spend their wealth in the Cause of Allah, and do not follow up their gifts with reminders of their generosity or with injury, their reward is with their Lord. On them shall be no fear, nor shall they grieve. [2:262]

ٱلَّذِينَ يُنفِقُونَ أَمْوَٰلَهُمْ فِى سَبِيلِ ٱللَّهِ ثُمَّ لَا يُتْبِعُونَ مَآ أَنفَقُوا۟ مَنًّا وَلَآ أَذًى لَّهُمْ أَجْرُهُمْ عِندَ رَبِّهِمْ وَلَا خَوْفٌ عَلَيْهِمْ وَلَا هُمْ يَحْزَنُونَ ۝

This is another example of how he would not own much besides what would bring him nearer to Allāh, and his generosity in giving away anything he had, no matter how small, and this is from the clearest manifestations of sincerity towards Allāh. So, Glorified is the One who leads whom He Wills to what He Wills. I was also told by a trustworthy friend that the Shaykh (may Allāh be Pleased with him) never turned back anyone who would ask him for something he wrote. Rather, he would have him go and choose for himself what he wanted. One time, a man came and asked him for a book that would benefit him. So, he ordered him to enter his library and choose what he wanted.

So, the man saw an expensive Mushaf between the Shaykh's books, took it, and left. Some of those present criticized the Shaykh for this, and he said: "Is it proper of me that I prevent him from something he has asked for? Leave him, as he might benefit from it." And the Shaykh (may Allāh be Pleased with him) was always very harsh against those who would prevent someone from a book of knowledge after he had asked for it, saying: "Knowledge should not be held back from the one who seeks it."

And from his generosity was that he never once looked with desire towards a position of leadership or authority.

These examples of his generosity are enough for the one who wants to follow in his footsteps.

O you who have believed, do not invalidate your charities with reminders or injury as does one who spends his wealth [only] to be seen by the people and does not believe in Allah and the Last Day. His example is like that of a [large] smooth stone upon which is dust and is hit by a downpour that leaves it bare. They are unable [to keep] anything of what they have earned. And Allah does not guide the disbelieving people. [2:264]

يَٰٓأَيُّهَا ٱلَّذِينَ ءَامَنُواْ لَا تُبْطِلُواْ صَدَقَٰتِكُم بِٱلْمَنِّ وَٱلْأَذَىٰ كَٱلَّذِى يُنفِقُ مَالَهُۥ رِئَآءَ ٱلنَّاسِ وَلَا يُؤْمِنُ بِٱللَّهِ وَٱلْيَوْمِ ٱلْءَاخِرِ ۖ فَمَثَلُهُۥ كَمَثَلِ صَفْوَانٍ عَلَيْهِ تُرَابٌ فَأَصَابَهُۥ وَابِلٌ فَتَرَكَهُۥ صَلْدًا ۖ لَّا يَقْدِرُونَ عَلَىٰ شَىْءٍ مِّمَّا كَسَبُواْ ۗ وَٱللَّهُ لَا يَهْدِى ٱلْقَوْمَ ٱلْكَٰفِرِينَ ﴿٢٦٤﴾

His Strength and Bravery

Seek (beneficial) knowledge, because seeking it for the sake of Allah is a worship. And knowing it makes you more God-fearing; and searching for it is jihad, teaching it to those who do not know is charity, reviewing and learning it more is like tasbeeh. Through knowledge Allah will be known and worshiped.

He (may Allāh be Pleased with him) was from the bravest of people and had the strongest heart. I never saw anyone who stood firmer than he did, or was more focused in Jihād against the enemy than he was. He would engage in Jihād for Allāh with his heart, tongue, and hand, and he would not fear the blame of the blamers instead of Allāh.

Many people told me that if the Shaykh (may Allāh be Pleased with him) was in the trenches with the Muslims, he was the one who would keep them firm and solid. If he saw some of the troops wavering, softening up, or showing signs of cowardice, he was the one who would encourage them, keep them firm, higher their morale, and give them glad tidings, and he would promise them victory, success, and war booty, and he would remind them of the virtues of Jihād and the Mujāhidīn and how Allāh descends tranquility upon them. If he mounted a horse, he would control it with expertise and precision, speeding into the midst of the enemy with utmost bravery and courage. He would sit on his horse like the firmest of knights, and would yell a takbīr that would damage the enemy more than any attack would, and he would roam around them like a man who did not fear death.

They relate that they saw him during the conquest of 'Akkah, a city in north-western Palestine, display bravery that one could not even begin to describe, and that he was the reason that the Muslims ended up taking it, because of his deeds, advice, and sharp perception.

And when the Sultān Ghāzān took over Damascus, the king of the Georgians accepted a large sum of wealth from him in order that he be given free reign to attack the Muslims of Damascus. When the Shaykh learned of this, he immediately got up and roused the Muslims' desire for martyrdom, and promised them victory, establishment, security, and the disappearance of their fears. So, a group of the leaders of the society went out with Ibn Taymiyyah to meet Sultān Ghāzān. When he saw them, he said: "Who are these people?" It was said to him:

"They are the leaders of Damascus." So, he allowed them to enter, and they sat in front of him. The Shaykh was the first to enter, and when Ghāzān first saw him, he immediately felt a deep love for him in his heart, and sat him down close to him.

The first thing the Shaykh addressed was the issue of having the treacherous Georgian king rule over the Muslims and giving him such vast sums of wealth. He reminded Ghāzān of the sacredness of Muslim blood and admonished him. Ghāzān responded with submission, and this became the reason that the blood of the Muslims was preserved, and their women and children protected. I was informed by a trustworthy friend that Shaykh Wajīh ad-Dīn bin al- Manjā (may Allāh have Mercy on him) said:

"I was with the Shaykh at this meeting, and he would remind the Sultān of the words of Allāh and His Messenger, peace and blessings be upon him, regarding justice, and he would raise his voice while talking to the point that the Sultān was down on his knees. He kept getting closer and closer to him during his talk that his knees almost touched the Sultān's, with the Sultān fully attentive to him the entire time, listening to every word, and never turning away. Because of the immense love and respect that Allāh had placed in the Sultān's heart for Ibn Taymiyyah, he asked those present: "Who is this man? I have never seen anyone like him or with a heart as firm as his, not have I been affected by any words as I have been by his, nor have I ever been as submissive to anyone as I have been to him." So, he was told of who he was, and was informed of his knowledge and deeds, and the Shaykh told the translator to tell Ghāzān:

"You claim to be a Muslim, and that you have judges, scholars, callers to the prayer - from what we have been told - and you still invaded us. Your father and grandfather were disbelievers, and they never did what you have done! We had a pact which we kept, and you broke your pact. You made a promise, and broke your promise." The Sultān told him: "If you like, I will make you the ruler of the land of your forefathers, Harrān, and you can move to it." Ibn Taymiyyah said: "By Allāh, I will never leave the land that Ibrāhīm (peace be upon him) migrated to and exchange it for another home."

So, he left this meeting with honor. He had a pure intention when putting himself on the line to preserve the blood of the Muslims, and Allāh gave him what he sought. This was also the reason for most of the Muslim prisoners being freed from the hands of the Mongols and returned to their families. These are all from his great displays of bravery and firmness. He would always say: "No man fears other than Allāh except that he has a sick heart. A man complained to Ahmad bin Hambal of his fear of some of the rulers, and Ahmad said: "If you were healthy, you would not fear anyone," meaning that his fear was the result of his heart being devoid of health."

I was told that when the Shaykh was summoned to meet the Sultān Nāsir Muhammad, he was told: "I am told that the people obey you, and that you seek a position of authority." The Shaykh was not intimidated by him, and said to him with a firm heart and a loud voice: "I said this? By Allāh, your kingdom and the kingdom of the Mongols are worth nothing to me."

The Sultān smiled at these words, and answered him based on the love and respect that Allāh had placed in his heart: "By Allāh, you are a truthful man, and the one who told me this about you is a liar," and the love of Ibn Taymiyyah was forever engrained in his heart. Were it not for this love, he would have killed him long ago due to the various lies he was told about him from those who were outwardly righteous and inwardly corrupt and ignorant.

And the innovators, people of desires, and those who traded their religion for the dunyā continued to cooperate with each other in their enmity towards him, exerting their efforts in harming him, lying upon him, ascribing to him what he would never say or write in a book or a fatwā, and what would never be heard from him in a gathering.

Do they not think that Allāh will ask them about all of this and take them to account for it? Have they not heard His Saying:

And We have already created man and know what his soul whispers to him, and We are closer to him than [his] jugular vein. [50:16]

$$\text{وَلَقَدْ خَلَقْنَا ٱلْإِنسَـٰنَ وَنَعْلَمُ مَا تُوَسْوِسُ بِهِۦ نَفْسُهُۥ ۖ وَنَحْنُ أَقْرَبُ إِلَيْهِ مِنْ حَبْلِ ٱلْوَرِيدِ ﴿١٦﴾}$$

When the two receivers receive, seated on the right and on the left. [50:17]

$$\text{إِذْ يَتَلَقَّى ٱلْمُتَلَقِّيَانِ عَنِ ٱلْيَمِينِ وَعَنِ ٱلشِّمَالِ قَعِيدٌ ﴿١٧﴾}$$

Man does not utter any word except that with him is an observer prepared [to record]. [50:18]

$$\text{مَّا يَلْفِظُ مِن قَوْلٍ إِلَّا لَدَيْهِ رَقِيبٌ عَتِيدٌ ﴿١٨﴾}$$

Indeed, by Allāh! However, their love of the dunyā over the Hereafter has overtaken them, just like their striving for the temporary life over the permanent life has. They envied him because of how he differed from them, because he hated and rejected what they sought, and because he loved what they abandoned and rejected. When Allāh knew his intentions compared to theirs, He did not allow them to gain victory over him, to the point that they never had a meeting or gathering with him except that Allāh caused him to defeat them, demolish their baseless arguments, and expose their evil plots with his tongue.

Patience Upon Hardship & Firmness Upon the Truth Until Death

The People of the Sunnah are the most knowledgeable of mankind concerning the truth, and the most merciful of the creation towards the rest of creation

He was the strongest, most esteemed, and firmest upon the truth of all the people of his time. He was the keenest to implement the truth, and no blame, words, or proof could dissuade him from this. Rather, if the truth became clear to him, he would bite onto it with his molar teeth, and would not turn to anyone who argued against it. Most of the people were united in their enmity for him, and most of those who hated him disguised themselves in the garb of the scholars and righteous folk, while they were in reality the quickest of people in running after the dunyā and turning away from the Hereafter.

The reason they hated him was because their only concern was to acquire positions of authority and leadership, and to have the people turn their heads towards them. They saw that Allāh had already elevated him to being the pinnacle in this by placing love and admiration for him in the hearts of everyone, while they had no share of this. So, the decided to become his enemies, and they filled their hearts with envy for him, attempting to hide this reality from the people so that they would not be exposed. They conspired to ascribe lies and falsehood to him and insulted him especially in the presence of the rulers, and they would criticize his verdicts declaring what was halāl and harām. So, they divided the hearts of the rulers with the lies they told about him, and they forget that they would eventually have to address all of this in front of the Judge of judges, as He will ask if they said all of this truthfully or unjustly, and He will reward the truthful with Paradise, and will take revenge upon the liars. Some of the people followed these lies simply as blind followers, and became oppressors in regards to the rights of this Imām, including those who had become slaves to the rulers, and would obey them and tell them what they wanted to hear in exchange for large sums of wealth. So, this viscous alliance consisted of many from all classes of the society, each having their own evil intentions in joining it.

With all of this, the more he saw their efforts to ruin his reputation, the more he strove to support and aide the truth, and the more effective and powerful his arguments and proofs against them became.

He was imprisoned many times, for many months and years, and he never turned his back and ran. His enemies tried to kill him many times, discussing their plans publicly and privately. But, Allāh proceeded to protect him from them. They thought that imprisoning him would relieve them of their worries. But, Allāh turned his imprisonment into a benefit and virtue, and brought out things on the day of his death that, had he been alive to see them, would have cooled his eyes.

Due to His Knowledge of his impending death, Allāh, the Exalted, relieved him of the worries of the people and caused him to go forth with the truth in the most beautiful manner, considering that he was imprisoned without any crime or offense. Rather, he was imprisoned for the sole reason that he was firm upon the truth.

This is how Allāh spread his knowledge throughout the world, and impressed countless minds with his style, filled countless books and pages with his writings, and suppressed through him the innovators and misguided followers of desires. These are the great results that the Lord of the Heavens brings about for those He Loves and Supports.

Allāh Made Him an Authority and a Clarifier of Truth and Falsehood

It is strange that a person may find it easy to protect himself from: eating Haraam, oppression and injustice, adultery, theft, drinking khamr (alcoholic drinks), and from unlawful looking, but it is hard for him to restrain the movement of his tongue. How often do we see people who are very cautious about falling into shameful deeds or injustice, but their tongue lashes against the living and the dead and they don't mind it?

Allāh made Ibn Taymiyyah a clarifier of truth and falsehood. This is something that is also well-known. He (may Allāh be Pleased with him) did not have a single book or fatwā except that he chose in it the strongest textual and logical proofs over all others, and backed up the word of truth with so many clear cut proofs and evidences that whoever comes across them with a pure conscience will have his heart cooled by them and will be utterly convinced that this is the undisputable truth. In all of his writings, you find that if the hadīth is authentic, he automatically takes it and acts upon it, and puts it forth over the opinion of any scholar or mujtahid.

The neutral observer will notice that his words are in accordance with the Qur'ān and Sunnah, and that he never deviates from them for the words of anyone else, no matter who that person might be, and he did not fear any ruler, authority, whip, or sword in doing this, and he would never abandon them for anyone's opinion. He held tightly to the firmest handhold, acting upon His Saying:

O you who have believed, obey Allah and obey the Messenger and those in authority among you. And if you disagree over anything, refer it to Allah and the Messenger, if you should believe in Allah and the Last Day. That is the best [way] and best in result. [4:59]

يَٰٓأَيُّهَا ٱلَّذِينَ ءَامَنُوٓاْ أَطِيعُواْ ٱللَّهَ وَأَطِيعُواْ ٱلرَّسُولَ وَأُوْلِى ٱلْأَمْرِ مِنكُمْ فَإِن تَنَٰزَعْتُمْ فِى شَىْءٍ فَرُدُّوهُ إِلَى ٱللَّهِ وَٱلرَّسُولِ إِن كُنتُمْ تُؤْمِنُونَ بِٱللَّهِ وَٱلْيَوْمِ ٱلْءَاخِرِ ۚ ذَٰلِكَ خَيْرٌ وَأَحْسَنُ تَأْوِيلًا ﴿٥٩﴾

And:

And in anything over which you disagree - its ruling is [to be referred] to Allah. [Say]: "That is Allah, my Lord; upon Him I have relied, and to Him I turn back." [42:10]

$$\text{وَمَا اخْتَلَفْتُمْ فِيهِ مِن شَيْءٍ فَحُكْمُهُ إِلَى اللَّهِ ۚ ذَٰلِكُمُ اللَّهُ رَبِّي عَلَيْهِ تَوَكَّلْتُ وَإِلَيْهِ أُنِيبُ ﴿١٠﴾}$$

I never heard of anyone who was as well-known as he was in his strict following of the Qur'ān and Sunnah, his efforts in extracting their meanings, and his acting based on their injunctions. He never came across an issue where the scholars had previously issued verdicts except that he chose the strongest and closest to the Qur'ān and Sunnah from them. Allāh blessed him with this characteristic, and He made him an authority for the people of his era. This was such that people from faraway lands would even send to him for fatāwā regarding their situations, and they would ask him to clarify for them confusion they had regarding this and that.

He often would cool their hearts with the most satisfying, solid answers, and he would always support his positions with the clearest proofs from the legitimate statements of the scholars, such that anyone with insight, intellect, and piety who abandoned his desires and came across them would accept them, and the truth would become clear to them. If someone was heard opposing him or attacking his honor, they would always turn out to be from those who were recognized by the general population as being evildoers, and whoever wishes to verify what I am saying, let him look with the eye of insight, as he will not find a scholar from any land who follows this Imām and recognizes the virtues and inspiration granted to him by Allāh, and praises him in every gathering except that behind such a scholar are the most strident followers of the Qur'ān and Sunnah, and the busiest in seeking the

Hereafter and the most desiring of it, and the farthest of them from avoiding or being ignorant of it. Likewise, you will also not see a single scholar opposing him and overtaken by envy of him except that he is the keenest of them in gathering the delights of the dunyā, the greatest of them in showing off and seeking praise, the most indecent of them in manners, the most cooperative with the oppressors in their plots, and the quickest of them to tell a lie.

If you look to those who loved him and those who hated him from the laymen, you will find them to be just as I have described the two groups of scholars above. I tried reflecting and thinking over what I have just said, and I saw that it is exactly as I have described. By Allāh, I do not hesitate in front of anyone in saying this, and whoever doubts what I am saying, let him think himself and he will see what I am saying if he removes from himself the covering of his desires. This is not the case except because of what Allāh Knew of the pure conscience of this Imām, and his sincerity and sacrifice in seeking the Pleasure of his Lord and following the Sunnah of His Prophet (peace be upon him, his Household, and Companions). When he came to his Lord with a pure heart [attached to Allah Alone and none else, worshipping none but Allah Alone true Islamic Monothcism, pure from the filth of polytheism]. [37:84]

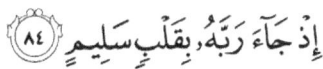

And those who believe and do righteous deeds - We will surely remove from them their misdeeds and will surely reward them according to the best of what they used to do. [29:7]

وَٱلَّذِينَ ءَامَنُوا۟ وَعَمِلُوا۟ ٱلصَّٰلِحَٰتِ لَنُكَفِّرَنَّ عَنْهُمْ سَيِّـَٔاتِهِمْ وَلَنَجْزِيَنَّهُمْ أَحْسَنَ ٱلَّذِى كَانُوا۟ يَعْمَلُونَ ﴿٧﴾

And those who believe and do righteous deeds - We will surely admit them among the righteous [into Paradise]. [29:9]

وَٱلَّذِينَ ءَامَنُوا۟ وَعَمِلُوا۟ ٱلصَّٰلِحَٰتِ لَنُدْخِلَنَّهُمْ فِى ٱلصَّٰلِحِينَ ﴿٩﴾

And Allah will surely make evident those who believe, and He will surely make evident the hypocrites. [29:11]

وَلَيَعْلَمَنَّ ٱللَّهُ ٱلَّذِينَ ءَامَنُوا۟ وَلَيَعْلَمَنَّ ٱلْمُنَٰفِقِينَ ﴿١١﴾

He punishes whom He wills and has mercy upon whom He wills, and to Him you will be returned. [29:21]

يُعَذِّبُ مَن يَشَآءُ وَيَرْحَمُ مَن يَشَآءُ وَإِلَيْهِ تُقْلَبُونَ ﴿٢١﴾

When you are in distress, say: "My Lord, give me victory and support me against the thalemeen (corrupting people)."

قَالَ رَبِّ ٱنصُرْنِى عَلَى ٱلْقَوْمِ ٱلْمُفْسِدِينَ ﴿٣٠﴾

His Death and the Immense Crowd That Attended His Funeral

Prophet Muhammad, peace and blessings be upon him said: "I leave behind me two things, The Quran and My Sunnah and if you follow these you will never go astray."

More than one person who was present in Damascus when he died told me that the Shaykh (may Allāh be Pleased with him) became sick for a few days, and the writer Shams ad-Dīn al-Wazīr was in Damascus at the time. So, when he knew that the Shaykh was sick, he asked to visit him. The Shaykh gave him permission to do so, and he sat with him and apologized to him for any shortcomings from his side in regards to the rights of the Shaykh. So, the Shaykh replied to him by saying:

"I have forgiven you and all of my enemies who did not know that I was following the truth. I have forgiven King Nāsir for imprisoning me, because he did this based on what he believed from others and not from his own intent, and he is excused for this, as Allāh Knows that he is not one to do this on his own. I have forgiven everyone who had some conflict with me except those who are enemies to Allāh and His Messenger."

Kind speech and forgiveness are better than charity followed by injury. And Allah is Free of need and Forbearing. [2:263]

﴿ قَوْلٌ مَّعْرُوفٌ وَمَغْفِرَةٌ خَيْرٌ مِّن صَدَقَةٍ يَتْبَعُهَا أَذًى وَٱللَّهُ غَنِىٌّ حَلِيمٌ ﴾ ﴿٢٦٣﴾

No blame will there be upon you today. Allah will forgive you; and He is the most merciful of the merciful. [20:92]

قَالَ لَا تَثْرِيبَ عَلَيْكُمُ ٱلْيَوْمَ يَغْفِرُ ٱللَّهُ لَكُمْ وَهُوَ أَرْحَمُ ٱلرَّاحِمِينَ ﴿٩٢﴾

The Shaykh remained until the night of the 22nd of the sacred month of Dhu al-Qi'dah of the year 728 H, 50 and he then proceeded to the Mercy and Pleasure of Allāh - the Exalted - the next morning doing what he was always doing: struggling for Allāh while patient, awaiting his reward, and not showing the slightest bit of cowardice, weakness, or wavering. Rather, when he died, he was busy with Allāh in exclusion to everything else.

They say that as soon as the people heard of his death, everyone living in Damascus came to pray over him. Everyone put aside whatever they were doing - closing shops, halting their livelihood and work - and all of the authorities, governors, scholars, jurists, soldiers, generals, men, women, and children from all levels of the society came out for his funeral.

To my knowledge, almost every person stayed at his funeral except for 3 people who were known for their enmity towards the Shaykh. They ran away and hid themselves out of fear that if they went out, the people would throw stones at them.

So, he (may Allāh be Pleased with him) was washed and shrouded. When he was being washed, the people crowded around so that they would each get some of the water that fell away from his body. Then, he was brought out for his janāzah. As soon as the people saw him, they crowded around him from every corner of the city to seek the blessing of being there. This was to the point that it was feared that he would fall to the ground before arriving at his grave.

The authorities gathered around where his body was and held the crowds back to prevent it from falling, as they began pushing and shoving each other viscously. They kept pushing them back from the janāzah with all their might, and this only served to increase the crowd's force. He was finally brought into the Umayyid Mosque, and despite the fact that it was thought that there would be enough space for everyone, there still remained a large group of people outside. So, they prayed over him (may Allāh be Pleased with him) in the mosque, and he was then carried by the hands of the nobles and citizens of Damascus until he was finally placed in a wide hole in the ground, and the rest of the people prayed over him there. One of those present said: "I prayed over him in the mosque, and I also had someone save me a spot to pray over him in the center of Damascus, as I wanted to see the massive amount of people.

So, while I was praying, I kept looking left and right, and I could not see where the crowd ended! Rather, I saw that the people had taken up every single bit of space that could be taken."

A group of those who were present that day agreed that upon seeing the number of people who prayed over him that day, they easily exceeded 500,000. The experts in history say that they never heard of a funeral prayer that was as big as this except that of al-Imām Ahmad bin Hambal (may Allāh be Pleased with him). Shams ad-Dīn al-Wazīr finally appeared when he was brought to his grave, as he had not been present before, and he and the governors with him prayed over Ibn Taymiyyah.

No janāzah was ever seen evoking such feelings of respect, veneration, esteem, glorification, and praise from the people, and this was all due to the his knowledge, deeds, zuhd, worship, rejection of the dunyā, preoccupation with the Hereafter, his poverty, concern, generosity, patience, firmness, courage, straightforwardness in speaking the truth, harshness against the enemies of Allāh and His Messenger and deviants from His Religion, supporting Allāh and His Messenger, peace and blessings be upon him, and His Religion, his humility, generosity, honor, and respect towards the awliyā' of Allāh, his lack of attention to the worldly delights, his extreme desire for the Hereafter, and his constant pursuit of it. And you would hear of these things and more from men, women, and children, and they would all praise him for what that they knew of him.

He was buried that day (may Allāh be Pleased with him and allow us to be granted similar blessings once again). The people then began gathering from the various villages and towns riding and on foot to pray in turns over his grave, and whenever news of his death reached a certain land, they would offer the prayer in absentia for him in all of its mosques, especially in the towns and villages of Egypt, Shām, Iraq, Tabrīz, al-Basrah, etc.

And the Qur'ān was completed for him more times than can be counted in many places during the days and nights following his death, especially in Syria, Egypt, Iraq, Tabrīz, al-Basrah, etc. to the point that reciting the Qur'ān for him became a habit for the people, and copies of the Mushaf would be passed around for them to read for him.

This was all because of what they felt they owed the Shaykh (may Allāh be Pleased with him) for guiding them to the truth and the correct methodology with the clear, evident textual and intellectual proofs, especially in regards to the principles of the Religion. Allāh blessed the people in this era in which innovations emerged that killed off the sunan, and the majority of its people were drowning in innovation and the harām in a way they did not even realize! And Allāh blessed them by having him clarify the principles of the Religion and the true and correct belief for them, as well as his distinguishing refutation of the innovators in a way that has so far remained unsurpassed. This was all done by his tongue, his pen, his books, and the principles he abided by that conformed to the truth and its implications, as well as the clear, simple textual and intellectual proofs he presented that none of the philosophers or debaters could even come close to. He did all of this until he was able to assert his absolute authority and dominance over every innovator, and was able to expose and wipe out the doubts of those who espoused and wished to spread them.

So, may Allāh reward him with the best of rewards on behalf of Islām and the Muslims, and Glorified is the One who gave him what he had, granted him the best guidance to what he was guided to, and provided him with the most beautiful patience until he died, and may He be Pleased with him, and may He grant us and all the Muslims a life and death that is in accordance with the Qurān and Sunnah until we meet Him, and cause us to hold firmly to them in all that they contain.

www.ingramcontent.com/pod-product-compliance
Lightning Source LLC
Chambersburg PA
CBHW071854070526
44583CB00016B/1684